The Cold Stones of Feeling

Also by T M Collins

Poetry

My Poetry (1986)
The Poetic Totem (1990)
Yabby Creek (1997)
House of Voices (1998)
The Ruined Room (2000, 2001)
Along the Lip's Edge (2006)
The Crooked Floor (2009)

Fiction
Until a Shrimp Learns to Whistle (2006, 2019)

T M Collins

The Cold Stones of Feeling

To the memory of my father
Maurice John Collins

Never tell me that not one star of all
That slip from heaven at night and softly fall
Has been picked up with stones to build a wall.

'A Star in a Stone-Boat' – Robert Frost

The Cold Stones of Feeling
ISBN 978 1 76041 995 0
Copyright © text T M Collins 2020
Cover photo: Bridget Collins

First published 2020 by
GINNINDERRA PRESS
PO Box 3461 Port Adelaide 5015
www.ginninderrapress.com.au

Contents

Woodsmoke and Ash	7
A Litter of Seven	10
Teardrops on a Feather	13
Lions and Inscriptions	15
Like a Diving Bell Fathom Dropping	17
The Cold Stones of Feeling	20
High Country, Australian Alps	22
Stage Whispers	24
Ticking Again	26
Detention	28
The Trawler	29
Nacht und Nebel	31
The Bat, the Bell, the Bird and the Body	34
You Are Gone	36
Summer Night Writing	37
Fragments	39
Chateau de Lavigny, Switzerland	40
Salute	41
The Long House	43
Fallen Leaves	44
Viewing Room	46
The Logger's Cabin	47
Faded Roses and Rusted Rivets	49
The Rhythm Line	50
Compass	52
The Octopus	54
On the Road Outside Comet	55
A Blue Tinge in the Glass	59
Night Has No Memory	61
Summer City Cycle	63

Night Loneliness	64
Dead Possum	65
Fumes Caught in a Net	67
Just South of Echo	73
The Woodblock Cutter	75
It's Just a Photograph	78
The Watcher	79
Writing	80
Camping	81
Old Photograph	82
The Zoo	84
That Bike	85
Frame our Determination	86
Acknowledgements	89

Woodsmoke and Ash

for my father

The boy wants to catch a fish
with black crystal eyes and
arched feathered spines up
its back with a tail flecked in
Nature's hued colours.

He needs to feel the
wet silver fur of scales,
the smell of woodsmoke and ash
as the fish is laid out flat
on a steel plate of dark.

He watches the scar
on the water's surface,
at the line-point ripples cobble out,
vibrating floating circles pronouncing
silent echoes under the skinniness
of the moon's fine filigree blanket.

Fish scorn the hook, fictive intent in
their wilful stuck-open eyes.

He waits for the mashing body
movements relayed jerkingly
along the line and hopes to hear
a forlorn nightbird sing as his
eyes and ears reel that fish in,
the wet line slicing, sandering a
faint joint line crease in water.

Fish tunnel, stop, go in all other
directions, a batsman's cricket wheel score.

He feels the tugs and flogs, the line limp,
then wet sandbag heavy then limp, and
he hopes it won't flog once too often,
the line's severed length gone lifeless
on the water's black back.

Fish gently zigzag, drift, silk rippling
underwater, patrolling, easing calmness
with each shiny flick fin flick.

Water striates blue black on silver as
behind the jetty, the road and town
outskirts are oddly historic and poetic.

At this petty point of global landscape time
is hoarded on blackened trains out of town –
all that matters is the sudden suicide tug of line.

The boy wears his father's old pelt hat
('21 rabbit pelts went into this hat, son'),
punch-drunk soft, worn and floppy,
a thumb hold hole through the front point
and in the shallowed brim the
sweaty stains of splintered years
of hard work and tonight in that
brim's slight gutter some moonlight slept.

He hears his father's mutter on the breeze,
a soft quelling voice like drifting ash and
that breeze, distant uilleann pipes
tingling the cold from his lips.

The line sings at the water's resting ear,
the moon eats darkness, the sky is
arched buckled back, harpooned into
deepest night and the stars, little query
lights, click and tink time, on and off.

He places two slivered fillets on
blackened steel and begins pattering,
turning, heat sizzling flesh, scorching
pink to white while the constant
bat-squeak of wood under flame
hangs cool in the night air.

Death and darkness are his company
tonight – a sad soliloquy – alone in a
wooded clearing edge-near water
orange-lit tree lichen watches the
flagellating flames reflect upwards into
the boy's squinting smoke-washed eyes.

Behind the cunning of the boy's thoughts,
memories toil over like mould growing old,
he wipes tears as an owl scarecrowing
night blinks once and a train drags
blackened time out of town.

A Litter of Seven

for my father

His determination for living
was flint-hard
yet in near death
his life was rudimentary.

His mangy hair
an unbridled mass of silver
his handshake long gone,
yet not his smile.

As a sparrow dawdled
old priest like at the
window edge
foamy lemony-coloured
clouds puppeted across
a blue wasteland and
a team of bay breezes
vague and serenely scattered
searched for venues to hang out in.

A nurse appeared briskly,
the doctor just arrived
lifting hope with a clipboard,
although he seemed disengaged,
almost eye-less in his reading of the charts
the nurse umbilical, tethered to his older knowledge.

The sun shawled warmly
about our shoulders, we watched
but we were already fixtures in
a moment after the event.

Echidna-spined with
grief and forlorned energy
I boarded the plane to a life
ceremony of emotions and
time bleached memories that
would sink and sack
continual tiredness into my face.

I tightened the strap,
over tightened it against his death
as the plane pulled itself upwards
closing the open white line down the centre
of the tarmac like a zipper on a mortuary bag,
I was pushed back into my seat as
he so often pushed back in pain.

Closing my eyes, I remembered
him saying to us at the dam's edge
'if there are bubbles it means
they've gone to heaven',
the hessian bag of kittens
sinking through the
slug coloured water
blistered with bubbles.

All day I've listened
to myself swallow,
a peculiar sound not
unlike the sound of
bubbles breaking the
water's surface.

Teardrops on a Feather

The boy begins cleaning, thinking of day –
ribbons of silver water and amethyst
flowers guard the inlet bank, then an owl
charms the night and starts a silent song
hollowed from darkness, its centred eyes,
dark-fruited berries as night creeps behind
blurred stars and rain stands like perspex.

His mother watches the clock slow turning.

He places each fillet on a chipped plate and
remembers kneeling, watching the rollered
box covered in the fine silk sash cloth of his
father's infant youth, watches it loosely
drawled, draped over the red wooden box.

Two thin fillets lined up on the plate,
the stove hotplate clinking heat, and then
drawn like a leaf on currented water the
box rolls to the heart of the flamed vault.

Turning the fish, flipping them back he
sees flames on silk riding quickly the fine
crease lines of soft ruffles, the flames
crackle and chuckle; content that they
are alive, they watch him as outside
shadows quiver dirty, expectant of more
light, not needing the greasy blackness
of evening, clouds with powder keg intentions
move into position and the moon sits
festooned with its grubby cables of light.

He hears his mother cough and spit, it is
now time to cordon off his thoughts, to
cook dinner and ignore her eyes, avoid
the slow tracer fire of her gaze following
his every movement.

He'll cook dinner knowing that she can
never explain.

He turns the memories over in his head,
these poor well-used thoughts have too often
been put to the lathe and plane and what
remains are but the feeble shavings of his life.

And like a teardrop on a feather nothing
much lasts in this life except memories.

Lions and Inscriptions

I heard the haunted voices of the ocean squabbling
and as decayed fear sat cross-legged on the watered rocks
a fog began circling the tipping end of the fishing rod.

A storm spectre in greyed overalls hunted the horizon
scatters of pilgrim piddle fish played about my feet and
my mind was wishing to be hooked, blindfolded away

from this turmoiled country with its strange language.
Fishing, me a hobo coastal dweller, my only weapons
for all to see – 2 antique fishing rods caught and detained

in an ivory-inlaid cedar cylinder – a talking point wherever
I travelled – my father's father's old competition rod holder
carved and oiled and stained, the surface glazed yet faded,

the wood's texture muddied and roasted by the angried sun,
oiled and inked by sweated use, salt infused by sanded beaches
and that inscription in old Hebrew, beautifully bent and

buckled letters carved fingernail tip deep into the soft grain.
But the pain of this place played out in the hurt of the
empty silence, life wrecked on this beach, nothing much

communicated here, questions were justly returned.
Tonight's night wallowed like a bustee water buffalo
yet the music of the surf like an ancient salved balm

soothed their stolen voices, crypted the memories steeped
away in sand, rock and plump-bobbed deep in stilled water.
Alone fishing, the pilgrim piddle fish nibbled at my feet

the line out cold and deep lingered at ease with the breeze
and the old man this evening at the bazaar selling me bait
with an insistent whisper, 'Lions once ran on that beach.'

The fog sag-eyed and old still hung grimly to the line.
I remembered Dad translating the mackling of letters
as I fingered magically the trenched words in wood.

'Believe, wherever you travel, in the elements, you must trust in you and us.'

Like a Diving Bell Fathom Dropping

After his death,
like a glass of dead water,
there it sat at his bedside table,
dust museumed around its base,
the little trinket box with the stringent
smell of purple gidgee and camphor laurel.

She said she hadn't the nerve to open it –
she told how he had toyed with the contents
everyday – she thought there could be no evil
in such a small thing – for all 56 years of mothering,
each given morning he'd sit on the bed and lift the lid
letting in a spike of air then slowly, methodically fidget
the contents – a ritual, like a spaceman's tight agenda of
trained and learned skills, the need to survive in outer space,
was it his safe flight each day – she was right I should not have
lifted the lid – his outer space was his daily routine and reaction to his
mind victuals; folded, settled and caved into this finger carved and palm
turned wooden display case historising six long decades of events, dreams,
captured caricatures, a stolid record, an encumbrance of abstract life, lived.

a 7-inch nail silver bluish with a sharp arrow point
a 1948 halfpenny with a buckled edge
5 paper clips all with apple flecks of rust
a folded wheat-coloured tissue with yellow red stains that had origamied each crease
a bus ticket West End to Enoggera with four equal perforations
a broken portion of tooth with E57 written in black ink below the good cusp side
one cufflink with an image of an antelope (gold on brown)
a pencil sharpener with curled feathered shavings inside
a classified clipping, *Sydney Morning Herald*, Korean War army number plates for sale
an obituary of Winston Churchill

a piece of white string tied in knots
a Queensland nut (macadamia) still in its shell casing
a Westgate Bridge opening ceremony bookmark
7 buttons – all different
a 1966 fifty-cent piece still wet with newness
a piece of white chalk
4 used matches the blackened crusted heads long gone

With a determination like a diving bell fathom dropping
I walked carrying the trinket box, sat on a hay bale at the
Gumdale Pony Club grounds, above clouds sheep walked
the impasto petrol blue sky, the air rinsed of dullness by
yesterday's showers but still the remnants of pewter storm
clouds dented and bruised the western horizon as a lexicon
of birds busy bodied adroitly in and out of the bewildered
shadows, the late morning sun watering the trees, the thriftiness
of the bay breeze drifting about like vague fish body-fiddling the
water's depths and my mind was off like a kite flying abstractly.

Noontime – ask questions of these objects, these things, did each have
a particular story, there was no belling narrative, nothing in there
ordered my thoughts, where was the alphabet of clues about his life,
were these all the victuals that he left, an utterly commonplace boxed
exhibit, what magnetic reason stood behind the existence of each object.

With a nearby tree propped horse shit shovel I dug a hole in the
middle of the quadrangle dressage area, placing four clods of
marl-coloured soil in a clear shopping bag, the box into the hole,
three clods of soil went back in unhappily, the fourth strewn in the bag.

At his home, in a flour sifter I sieved the fourth shovel load of soil, a falling mist of greyish brown, sifted it throughout the house letting it feather into the carpet, my shoes dusted in a temporary memory.

We were the arrow and the quiver, the mortar and the pestle, the cog and the sprocket, and lastly, the firm sound of pounding hooves.

The Cold Stones of Feeling

In the chapel my mind was a broken kaleidoscope of
mosaics of sad tincture, no colour seemed bright.
I could see my thoughts but they were all shattered.

He looked hauntingly at peace, that faultless smile
hiding a dossier of grins and the deep blue eyes.

Around a shawl of drooping trees people crowded and clutched,
bent spirited people, weighted by the cold stones of feeling,
listening to a filigree sermon, a sermon crisp yet lace-like,
beautiful words adorned with his honour explaining all.

A gravel rash sky, reddish streaks stricken in grey ash clouds,
the daylight moon just visible, I thought of the loneliness of the
reappearing moon and how no one owns the wind or its child,
the gentle breeze and no one ever owns any of our thoughts.
Invisible were these kingly thoughts and private sad me-things,
yet noticeable were the weeps and eye rubs in this August moment.

Turning from his headstone the black silk reaches of the river
creaked through the trees, this afternoon the wind was a sad optic
watching alone and as rain began grey-sheeting the sky there
was an ashen sadness in the rainy afternoon light.

The biography of a sad loss is bound up in the little things
of life, his voice, that gripping handshake, that smile,
the special urgency he gave to life and living
even in the most painful of times it was always
an eisteddfod moment where he gave to others.

He told me the detail was in the simple, in the little
aspects of everyday, in what appears to be insignificant.

A gust of wind thrilling a crow's wings or after early rain
how the footpath dries in odd portions giving an
impression of camouflage, dark grey and dirty white,
the woody crisp snap of the first bite of an apple, how
clouds move as if by puppet wires, how sheep slow walk,
a lizard sun drenched, its upcast eyes tight-lipped or
how bluish shadows can move like bruises across
or a school teacher's cut crystal voice extolling
or letter box lids mossed in dew or that same dew
whiskering a spider's web frosty, the ribbed fine
netting like iced quartz wormholes.

As the day dulled the sun crouched low in the sky,
the warm hiccupy heat gone, shadows shuddered,
wandered in the peaty blackness of evening as
clouds rubbed the sky of blueness and the moon
loaded with intent pulleyed up into the branches,
at the garden entrance – the rocks, stones were alive,
mansed in the landcsape living, audienced, watching
each day's ceremony, nothing is ever by happenstance.

A scuff of lightness in my step I walked with a strange sense
of calming, palming my grief and despair into a single sound,
one sound repeated, of his voice calling me, when I was child.

High Country, Australian Alps

Hunkered down in a gold miner's stone panelled hut
high on the carapace of a weather-whittled basalt out-drop
the hectoring wind and pestering rain, the schist grey sky,
the blistered Marsala inked sun drooling, watch-listening
the smouldering history of centuries of oldness, the timber
creak like sound of a rusted bent snaffle bit hung from the
hitching rail dribbling mist-dew to pumpkin-sized rocks

elbowed into soil like plump gourds beside a garnishing of
alpine wattle seeds spun legless up these uncaved slopes.
The tenacity of Nature, its struggle to keep isolation alone at
this spot, and below you, dogged ranges, mythed valleys
wetted sweeping hills, tussock strewn crags pilfering sunlight
from merino patches of snow, grounded grasses the colour of
cashmere, dirtied lambswool, alpaca, patiently warming the earth.

On a day when the wind is augmented by sharpened icicles
the hawk is hangered high in a curved over branch in a stand
of trees, the branches like tusks at the wind, making platitudes,
trite reminders that winter won't last, up here the wind can over
and up like buckling javelins ornamented with star clusters of ice
other days that wind is just the cooing of a harmless household
turtle dove and the bleached midday blue of the sky just roasts

but today as I patter-buffet the pan in the stream, the snaking
wobble of mercury sourcing my gold, the faint chink of little
grains on aluminium, the sky is a swollen flood-grey heavy.
There is a lazy ease to late afternoon, the temper like mortar
between two bricks gone off to the twenty-dollar-note-coloured west.
Up here there is safety – for when the cage is open, it isn't a cage.
Looking up, the peaked saddle of the roof is snow-loaded in

pristine white but there is that blacker weight before it slides.
Soon the winch will turn so that day cogs night chains yesterday
and in the morning the hawk will smoke the wind, and that wind for
tomorrow only will be silenced, benched and wired in an experiment,
the hawk sporting higher thermals with sun-chastened wings skippered.
Now as I pan with a pygmy breeze at my shoulder blades, a swath
of rain about to trounce in from the south, there is a thumbscrew of

heavied air about me as the varnish of night vanishes inwards, slowly
shuffling in like an uncalled witness and later this sated evening
darkness will drag her chains of undisturbed coldness chilling
across this landscape, the chimney will be piloting smoke and
and the hawk will be watch-listening; I'll be writing runes of ideas,
rereading aloud a race of words across down the page like fearful
slaves chain-locked, quarter stepping along a dirt dusted road, I'll be

pacing this enclave of wood, dirt, rock and steel high in the Alps,
rereading these words like spears thrown, I'll be watch-listening
the words and their thermals like the hawk and unlike the pearl diver
found face up floating in 1910 at Roebuck Bay, Western Australia…
two fistfuls of sand in his mouth, pearls shoved up his nose, in his ears.

And on his weathered gravestone the inscription:

'He gave up watch-listening; he was just another hawk in a cage'.

Stage Whispers

I'd read about his death on the stage
in front of the red velvet curtain, it was
always a dark theatre even with the lights
swallowing matinee and nightly expectation.

One night alone behind that curtain we spoke
closely of things that had been cut from our lives.

That night he ran his hand across the curtain back
over small carbuncles of caked on dust, accumulated
from years of human humidity, dust that listened.

Now I pick at the memory, little dried dust hillocks
stuck long hard to the canvas-backed curtain, I pick.

Often on a Sunday after a rehearsal the young lads
would broom the red velvet curtain, the front side
billowing, buffeting with the air conditioning's breath.

But that backside was torpored in hesitation, heavied in
memory, long days, nights without searching stage lights.

As we spoke closely that night I scratched at a hillock,
not completely listening to his words for his voice was
so soft and pleasing like a gentle breeze that just ups over
a sun baked ridge and briefly fans you then loses itself.

There was this feathering of fine silt drifting below
my fingers as he talked to me about things, I was divorced
from everything, except the curtain's slight swayed movement.

There was an art deco-ness to his hands as he spoke, they offered up his words in encased gestures, feelings, often sensations I felt through my whole body and always there was this brown robed backstage glow and a silly silence like it did not know what to do with what it was seeing.

Most men I'd known had stiff walking stick arms full of sinew and urgent release, his hands and arms worked with his words, played with his voice like someone trying slowly to place silver silk over gently rippling waters.

As he talked a yellowed moth above his right shoulder walked backwards up a curtain fold, and for a funny tiny second I thought of the manufactured air in this his theatre, and as air has no memory I thought about how the moth would live here, alone, in this place, his place.

Ticking Again

Each blade moves lost shadow
the wind works as a mood
the ticking harmonics of heat
turning down, starving and
the ashed landscape reeking
of dead flame, boned in black.

Samplings of weak sunlight
vein the powdered paddock
as somewhere off rifle fire
re-echoes like nails splitting
hardwood, the bop-tick
sound, so clean and heavy.

Walking on the ashen-flaked carpet,
the short sibilant sound of puffs
of charcoaled matter ink-mist up as
hessian sacks frayed, singed, useless
stray the fence line, the barbed wire
still stinging and sulking from the heat.

Everything seems stolen of
time and purpose except the
bickering storm clouds that spot
stain, token the sky, the weakened
sky blistered and scuffed from the
torn and stale smoke bloom.

The blather of returning birds
with thirsted wings and the
sand and glue of humidity as the
the old steel windmill boxed in
stilled sleep for days begins
ticking again like slow footsteps.

Detention

for Robert John
'All colours will agree in the dark' – Francis Bacon

From where he is
the Bridge of Teal
affords no real view
it is just a grey
cantilever bridge

but its play with the
afternoon sun gives
him its name, those
girders and arches
become watered in

teal but it is only
for an hour or more
while the sun monkeys
about in that part of
the sky, in winter with

the sun trapezing on
the lower branches it is
shrouded and dyed so
beautifully for longer,
perhaps four hours or more.

'The purest and most thoughtful minds
Are those which love colour the most.' – John Ruskin

The Trawler

Needle trembling fingers and the piercing of my chest, the sloping deck, the sun at my left cheek, the waves pillow-fighting the hull, waterbirds winging off in laughter heading for the Andaman Sea. Angry from the

jacked-up chain gang waves ocean spray pedestals a seagull mid-air, its body a fluttering water sculpture of indecision. This afternoon the wind is a bad lyric travelling alone while danger courts its shadow.

The drug's pain-free promise chugs me into a swirl of fuzzy thoughts, my injured body propped up sitting on the cold wet ridden, salt washed, wooden warped greyed planks that have seen many a fool try to play,

ply the ocean's resources like a game of Monopoly and almost every week there's an injury and the question 'is it worth it' – you're not paid until the work is fully done, the deck polished shot clean; the

vessel parked three a girth in the river's cyclone ulcerated gut mouth, the catch packed, robbed north to the Asian market, and over all noise the first mate's grog-gravelled voice; he's called Drag, shot a drag queen

in King's Cross, did eleven years in the Commonwealth Hotel, and he's shouting rock song like 'not two hits, just one', my cold thoughts jump, the pumping veins at my neck and temple pulse in tune with the stuff's

slow ammeter ticking of numbness; it takes hold like a stay wire tightening, then nothing except the buffeting of water against hull, the trampolining of the boat being hypnotised, the sun up, the sun down, up, down, sea foam

remnants drying about my feet as I begin to froth at the mouth, later being the dried satin powder moth wing dustings of the moment, my mind now a medicated high beam, solid and filmic, my drug-heavied eyes watching

the rusted rail of the boat cut a split along the sky's greying waist, then
impishly my mind drifts from the frippery of the day, my memory as
blank and bleak as a washed-up aqualung on an empty beach, and in

full daylight, half-sleep, then in thickening dark, a dark where the moon
and its sad meltings had gone and in dark's middle shadow – the fear inked
into capillaries, into veins, stained deep in arteries, curdling and curling

towards my heart, my blood like black silk pulled from brown mud,
my eyes see nothing but a shawl of pitch; my eyes trace blackness,
it is in these surreal moments that I hope, no time for bent spirited

logic, rabbit's feet, shark's teeth or grime-smeared gold crosses, I listen
for the first crush of something, a crick, a shouldering of air, a cat-wind –
some thin warmth, a slight smouldering heat that will pass around me, my

body like a damaged stile gate, I wait the cold inching in of darkness
the incident refilmed again and again in the darkened trench of my
thinking, only the sounds of voices spilling the night air, loud voices

around me on the deck, I'm propped up sitting, my burlap head cap dripping
wet, I'm shoved wits full of two hits of morphine, while the voice's bodies
work the ocean's belly, with witches and daisies in the whites of my eyes

I listen to the pray of the waves in the ocean's hymn, that continual pattern
of calmness, it is like being on a time train to where you've just been,
death's dark wires wield their fairing current post to post as the train below

is oblivious to life's dark awakenings, and I'm still on deck as is the rule,
being watched, not below in a rocking sweat-streaked sea hammock, my
troubling body becoming rotting nuisance compost in stinking heated heat.

Nacht und Nebel

for Lilly Brett

'Under a full moon on a distant
Tideless shore I hear men shouting' – Shurin

Tonight at the quietude of this beach, like an old hawk's
nest in the fork of a dead tree all of time waits here.

My feet suckered, plugged in wet sand,
warm and cool throbbing water frothing about.

Sea lice putt about in a bucket of stale surf water
snorkelling the meniscus.

My reflexes puppet-wired to capture each transaction
of coded movement along the monofilament line.

Cauldroned on this witchless beach under a silicon-crusted
scorched black sky with old darkness tricked and tethered,
the foul, fierce Macbethed weather gone, my thoughts, my
senses aged and eyeless, my head helmeted by strychnine memories.

Moonshine decanted through clods of laundried clouds illuminates my middle
finger green inked vertically with Aussie as it triggers the wet breeze twinging line.

That breeze canoes in towing a thin veil of fog.

The sound of motioned water being vacuumed out, the popping and
bubbling, the feathering taps and bounces like dry drum skin beats,
the leaving surge pimpling the sand tanned with foamed fossil resins,
those drumbeat echoes trying to dream and ink into my head.

Stars humming their glow like old patrons in the darkened
reading room of the central Braille Library in Leipzig Germany.

Out past the line's trapped end the waves and their following hollows
resemble spotlit watered turquoise ditches of flattened grass.

Like graduates across a stage rehearsed the waves carriage in,
slow, precise and repentant for what they have seen.

With watered-down tact and less than abundant logic a nightbird folklores the
surface, thinking of ancient fish it wood turns itself for another low-angled flyover.

Like long-forgotten airport deliveries to a hobbled foreign country other stray
birds bus about ignorant of time schedules silently moving, low, slow and heavy.

I prune and cage my imagination, tighten and stiffen my concentration
like a coastal towns flood barriers ready, the coal vein of my heart
a solid yipping metronome beat like a hunting, craving pulse.

Crabs dance the wheat-coloured floor – the surface scratched and marked
with their oiled muddied tracings, whip marks across the sand.

A spittle of mizzled rain begins knitting the sky dissolving the fog and
pestering the water's surface into a massaged area of settling suck and throb.

In the bucket one lone louse tots around in bumping bobbing circles.

Away off in the nowhere distance a siren pockmarks night, the ear worming
of the sound like silver spurs heeled into the tough dark hide of existence.

Moving, towards my feet like a hovering stingray buffeting,
then suddenly settling a wax-papered diamond-shaped black,
white, green and red kite heavily watered, its spirit just dead
the long flat tail satined white like a tapeworm with the
blackened wordings.

Never forgotten, forever missing.

Night fishing at Haifa, Israel. *Nacht und Nebel* (Night and Fog) is
the title of a decree issued in 1941. It was Hitler's euphemism for
the way in which people suspected of crimes against occupying
forces would be dealt with. They would be spirited away into the
night and fog.

The Bat, the Bell, the Bird and the Body

for Andy Irons

Outside there is an admixture of emotion with milling sunlight
heating at the foot of the steps a browned black package,
an overnight-decayed Gould's wattled bat messaging the path
having been lost by off-course sickened flight, its fine nostril

hairs twitter alive, seemingly wet with the silicone gloss
of the day's watering and whispering sunlight, sunlight that
is sticking to everything like pasted glue as little dust motes
cable-car, ascend, descend and counterbalance themselves in

the beams of glow, realising they have no future or fortune
they rat about in the early morning ocean air watching as
I do the bird channelled wind shunting in from the south and
off to the west there is that limey light over the mountains

making woeful some traveller's family holiday with rain like
bullish needles to be thrown at will, like watermelon seeds
shot as pellets from a popgun, this afternoon levelling in
slanted then hunkering in for days, I am just pleased to sit,

the sun's flowering bulb of heat pulsing in finger-poking intensity
while way out, the deep-trenched water has caught an early poem
and the board riders smother-spot-bother the water's surface like
black grubs on coloured paddle popsticks and if you squint-eye,

narrowing your vision to a coned view you gather quickly the
mordant morsels of real life that are revalued here, this place
is important, as popcorn elephant clouds safari park the sky and
now the wild willowy wind submarines low and precise, patrolling,

and the leathered carcass of the bat tremors, just jiggers slightly
from side to side like the innards of a ruptured bagpipe still
somewhat alive with old pocketed and locked-in air, eking out
survival with every wind elbowed twitch but it is the heat that

turnstiles it into quick decay, into a wretched mass, leathered fur
leeching death as the stone church that dragged the polished pebbled
path up the hill two centuries ago closes in on itself as the angelus bell
sounds its passover of sentiment and as a paradise riflebird sews ancient

air travel stories in and out, over and across the belfry, the solid ground
below is winked in sunlight, pinpricks of shine teeter on grass tips,
this shine licks the pebbled path, polishes the wood of the trees, and
there is no noise, just sound, no silence just the cadence of things

moving, coming and going, drifting, working in fine adjustments, then
expectedly an ambulance crumbles the gravelled driveway, two young
paramedics rush 'inside', wide-eyed I nod at them, then watch the board
riders in the stilled distance seven or nine per wave stitching their way in.

You Are Gone

for Narelle Elizabeth Oliver

I remember the moon, its
gentle whip of silk flicking

across your bare shoulders as
the curtains rode the night

breeze, the rain clouds miming
sheep walks in the darkened

paddock, then to drift apart
again like foam scuttled by

ocean wave laps. And I
remember resting on my

back, you astride me, your
hair ends wet with sweat,

little stars gathered from
moonlight itching their

way along each thread of
silver brown, those ends touch

tickling my face as we kissed,
your body swanning over me.

Today I close my eyes and
feelings of you flicker

inside me as I realise you
are still my daily prayer.

Summer Night Writing

on a forlorn faded windowsill
a flame sits on a candle
the sparked flickers talking
dreams at the wick

the mailbox dewed in
night's overspill of darkness

the road hangs off the yard
like a detached darkened slope
down and out, offering nothing

there is a shuffle of coolness
through that window ajar
curtains sheltering unpaid humidity

flying foxes black flag the
moonless sky, clouds filthy as
dishcloths pile here and there
making a mess of the night

stars amputation points
charged raw and radioactive
haemorrhage light and laughter

an owl reads the stars
but there is nothing new
in their narrative connections

a cat missing history and time
moves silently like a half-breath

the flame bends a little, the
wick pulls it upright once more

on a fence a possum times and marks
weather with its disgruntled presence
leaving a scattering of assessment

the yellow crime of wick and flame continues
the cat no longer chasing its Celtic sins sits
as stardust spores settle on its furred coat

night creeps as shadows float and ruffle
leaving faint charcoal buffings, bloodlines
for thought, pulses of language offer up
a sweltering of drip-fed thinking.

Fragments

for Dad

faultless in his smile
a smile always freshly minted
a smile with a dossier of grins –
wry, sombre, questioning

always with an
Irishman's humour

his handshake
grip-arresting

his lapis lazuli eyes, deep
Indian Ocean blue

his face handsome
at 82

with no asperity
he'd say
'don't brisk me'

but now he is ballast in his bed
making silence with life

hauntingly at peace, a fleet of arrows
forever arching across the sky, lost.

Chateau de Lavigny, Switzerland

Midday's satin glow
sneaks through day's
dreamy turnstile.

The breeze up from
Lake Geneva
chuckles as it
moisturises the earth.

Clouds clean and swab
the blue-tiled roof as I sit
on a rampart of aged stone,
anciently coloured in grey,
spin drifted in charcoal and
pinpricked with featherings
of turf-coloured mildew.

Tonight across Lac Leman
the textured mountains of France
will be sparked and lit by bonfires
dotting and edging the slopes
like miniature tiaras
for French National Day.

As I sit at the border of
one country and look
with gathered pride into
another, I am suddenly
aware of missing my
home country, Australia.

Salute

to Stewart

The loadmaster is dead.

We gather crammed in on a sunny day to celebrate the old Scot's life his son wears his kilt dabbing tears from his eyes as his wife touches gently his lower spine like young women in orchestra pits that finger violin strings when not meant to – readying, calming the instrument. Outside the day is chatty and full of grid lines of ease.

The loadmaster is dead.

I'm beside an old lady, full of wisdom and fear, she has what brought the loadmaster so swiftly down but her humour is still a Joshua moment. The eldest grandson chilled in a starched uniform, always combat ready walks robot like to the head of the coffin, his every joint oiled in respect and honour, simply he gives a hard arced salute to the wooden box, no emotion on his face as he walks back to the pew.

The loadmaster is dead.

As 67 old men file out of the their positions picking a greened sprig from a basket, the sheen, of a fear, of death, the love of a mate and that machine like regard at their bent shoulder blades, they are in a synchronicity – old men placing a sprig each on his coffin, and the old lady beside me bows her head heavily.

The loadmaster is dead.

As the bagpipes play 'Amazing Grace', dozens of swallows expelled by the shrill from the eaves of the crematorium battle fly the lawns, the coffin strolls forward, the pipe player hangs on the last few notes; Alex is resting, not listening, yet he arches his neck backwards to tell us one last story but as the first curtain closes, the second curtain follows quickly as if family, no bagpipes, no birds, they've settled, the old lady beside me just clasps her hands tightly and gently shakes her head.

The loadmaster is gone.

The Long House

for Willy Bach

One way in
one way out
try to leave.

Bach playing and
the 19-foot
table from Ceylon.

Kafka's portrait on
the wall and
dried flowers stuck
in a bucket.

A framed photo
of a handwritten
letter from a
Pol Pot refugee.

Arrived in rags
now a pharmacist,
a true refugee.

Incense burning in
every corner as
well as conversation.

Fallen Leaves

'I see men as trees, walking' – St Mark, New Testament

Today at the window watching for glimpses of
olive green growth sprouting from a 94-year-old
stag horn (*platycerium superbum*), an ancient
tree fern passed on from grandad to dad to me.

This bracket epiphyte of slow growth has been
wind-whipped and sun-scorched through the
long drought's open decree, every second day
feeding it Tasmanian bull kelp *(durvillaea potatorum)*
palmed in behind the curling brown fronds to
accelerate and warmly hasten its green moods.

Elbowing my eyes upwards I see the moon
halted on the sky like a congealed milky tear,
the old curse of the wind unwinding, unravelling
itself in tatters on the shaking aged branches.

It is a bleak day; the stars are hidden, buried
deep like cold old bone fragments as clouds
grey as mouse fur smoke across the sky.

Tonight rolling over to sleep I hear the gentle
piano thoughts, the ivory tinklings of inspiration
of the whistling trees and a few late-up birds
chatting, chittering about the colours of Nature,
colours so tight in their tincture, and all these
parts and colours are really minute engines
running, moving almost silently like a drum skin
quibbling or an aged bellows just breathing.

But soon this tree creature will be gone
choked of moisture by the drought's long
tight-fisted dryness and any recall of this
event will be lost in memory's crowded street.

Tomorrow will come and perhaps again
lightning will zip-piz about shaking its
aluminium flashing and a new wind with
a baby breeze hugging its back will tug at the
sheets of rain and I'll realise not to get so upset
about a dying tree fern when death so often
comes across the world like fallen leaves.

Platycerium Superbum is native to Australia.

Viewing Room

Through the bifold doors
of a just breathing house
full of saddlebag memories
and photos of him stationed
around the black piano, the
relatives and friends are tanked
in the sedative effect of a wake.

Like wet heavied kites lost of
their coloured drooping colours,
shouldering on downwards, the
atmosphere is vainly pillboxed.

Eel-like looks and chimpanzeed
gazes at the tiny half open casket,
and stray orphaned conversations.

The business of death and respect
is in the presence of his bedspread
with its stitched-on blue butterflies
draped over the dining room table
amputating any necessity for talk.

His lips soft velvet, chin chest-rested,
eyelids closed, leathered feathered thin.

Yet dead he seems alive, fresh, perhaps
his breath is prancing around the room.

As people attempt to whittle and carve,
treat and mend their memories of him an
old woman moving like a cat dusted in silk
bends in to kiss his paws and furred forehead.

The Logger's Cabin

There's a settle to the lighting,
part oil burn and fire glow wash,
the cabin walls are laced with this
loose-lipped light as worms of
warmth plug the gap-holes of
stalled time and outside ancient
winds sigh as they patrol, warning
the landscape of the coming storm,
a thoroughbred storm full of ice and
bat-winged snow, the hawking rocks
and buttocked boulders like dead
engines scattered in the ground, wait.

Shadows manifest themselves in the
forest as sounds, murmurs and mutters,
the trees sweat in the nape of the valley
as leaves jockey the branches ready,
the storm begins consigning its night
cargo of heavy early rain as charcoaled
patchings mark the area corralling the
cabin as gastric moon spray eats and
chews at the posts and boundary fences.

Bile bickering clouds junk in, the night sky is
brooding, wasting time before a rush hour
breeze hares in bringing with it steel-coloured
shadows inking the landscape as diesel fumes
of rain blot stain the old-teeth-coloured soil.

An owl badged on a high branch in this figment
of woodland timbers is scared, thinking of
where over the valley tombstoned tree stubs
brown pimple the ground, trees haikued at
the waist, dribbling sap like wasted semen
and the memoried echo of the noise of
the bucking, buckling tourniqueted chains.

Faded Roses and Rusted Rivets

'Even the signposts like grim liars' – 'Evening Mystery', Edmund Blunden

On a buckled Armco all that's visible is a
scraping of blue paint and six tarnished
rivet heads with raised lettering – TDL

and a bunch of withered flowers strapped
with tan masking tape to the post standing
bent and yet upright like a trauma memory.

On the little white cross it reads,

Ian,

You served your country and us.
Rest in eternal peace dear son, rest.

Love,

Mum & Dad.

And after a bit of searching
I found out TDL stands for
Transport Direct Link.

As cars approach
a head will often turn.

It has been 27 years
travelling this road.

The flowers now
rarely get replaced.

The Rhythm Line

The sun no longer with its wilful eye,
now the curious lip of moon
whispers hidden words at the
green dark trees, all upright,
stabbing the night air.

The eye does focus on height,
colour and movement.

The broken web in the night sky,
the stars – the unrubbed-out
portions of this fine web.

The patient breeze lifting bush smells
across the resting landscape.

And as I place another log,
rough and wind whittled
on the fire, you strip
and get into bed.

The tick and hum of night insects
quality-checks the beat of my heart and
somehow choruses the slow
rhythm line of your breathing.

You are settled, your wet hair
tails across both pillows.

Moonlight grazing for a glimpse wanders
through a gap in the shivering curtains.
Seconds pulse the minutes at hours
as I sit in the bedside chair with
my portmanteau of thoughts,
awaiting sleep.

Night shadows and
dim-lit skied lights,
woodsmoke and ash,
distant bird noises,
stiffly crisp sheets
and often tonight
I'll awake
and hear
the gentle timbre
of your breathing.

Compass

What is the purpose of a compass
but to show direction – one's bearings?
What direction was he doing in hospital?

The compass, an instrument, is not like a
torch which shows a path, a safe passage,
a front door at night or a cockroach stealing
darkness across an empty passageway.

You gave him a compass, his cold pleasure cash
registered away in a sigh, there in that bed with
lantern jaws, a mind havocked in fear, totally junked.

Was it about your need to give a trinket?
His favourite book was not *Gulliver's Travels*.

A falcon is not blindfolded in seeing its prey,
it has no quavering compass needle or torch
beam acuity to aide its fell swoop, nothing
to help change its innate architecture of flight.

The torch and compass are both
poetic forms of enlightenment, but
what of his rosary beads and missal?

Objects all have different weights, yes –
the missal was heavy with his faith, the
palm-polished amber beads light with hope.

What matchstick mentality – giving
a compass to a man dying in a hospital.

He couldn't walk, could hardly talk;
no desert, tundra track, Nullarbor or
Ranger lost, so why the compass?

The word compass in the dictionary
can mean to 'hem in', compass someone.

After he is fallen silent, his eyelids
lidded over, he lies beside his own life.

After his death – gathering his things,
the compass felt weighty, not waterlogged
or made of cheap lead, just solid, heavy with
hope and faith. My guess is, he hadn't yet let go.

The Octopus

Like shapeless
discarded pasta
on a tide-pleated beach,
the surf-draw unable
to retrieve her,
sunburnt and
water-wrinkled
she sank in the
afternoon mud-sand.

I crouched
touching her softness,
flesh, the feel of
cream silk, of
heavied sleep,
a wet life gone.

Above Pluto watched
the beach, thinking.

Needing a memory
I arm-carried her home
up the beach to sleep.

On the Road Outside Comet

'His life was a sort of dream, as are most
lives with the mainspring left out' – F. Scott Fitzgerald

'…you are as much at home as a hovering native bee,
or the wind, or death, or shaded trickling water.' – Les A. Murray

On a tar-patched strip of parched road up from a corrupt corner
he stands noticing landscape; the only firm sound the car engines
bumbling tune of rack snap crack of hot metal easing down,
as heat fumes neck upwards to scar tissue clouds.

Night-time will wear its tattered black coat, flecks of
white lining showing through, motheaten by landscape's
constant dry quips.

Soon the zodiac of stars, raindrops hung
on a blacked-out ferris wheel.

And other casual stars will ache their way to earth
tailing off behind Ibsen's stage curtain like specks of dust
dragging reflected light along their abraded edges.

He stands corralled by the cold sandstone touch of air,
the chip and scratch of starlight, one huge hand-pick constantly
sparking diamante chips across the night sky.

No opportunity or reason for colour, just specks of glow jam-packed
in the ash wall between the boulders of darkness.

Hundreds of miles midway between matchbox towns
the seconds fetter to minutes and he justly stands,
watching, thinking, his carousel of carded thoughts,
collated memories, a drabble of ideas about finding
a place to cruise his mind's worries, to graze
less traumatic times a while longer, to let the
tinder of his psyche settle not like letting rust
bubble and bauble through metal's cold flesh,
the crusty rust spots forever reappearing.

Nearby a leaf is harpooned on the rusty barbs of a barbed
wire fence, a fence where each strand is finger turn twisted
and bent and twisted back turned again to border, quarter and
dissect the *Terra Australis* emptiness two sunbaked centuries ago.

All seasons alive in death are bound up in the cradle of dryness of
that leaf as wire and wind wrestle the leaf in a triangular love affair.

Wind's shutter at any time will open and the leaf will be drawn
across the scene's surface to rest as Nature's collated litter.

Forever in his head the memories hold a mirror to thoughts,
looking at what might have been.

The sun's soul finally sinks darkening the charcoal-coloured sky.

Out here in the bush country the delinquency of nasty thoughts
should disappear.

On this gravel dirt dust shoulder lip verge of bandaged road
wondering about his future.

    Walk straight off
    into the bush
    where the waves
    of sneakish greenery
    and silent old wood
    will grow over you.

The road says nothing in either direction, the dotted line asleep,
bitumen relaxing, intoxicated from the daytime heat.

    Walk in, brisk past that tree with
    the whittle-wood curlings of bark
    peeling, peeling like old strappings
    of binging brown paper, stride in…

Consumed by heavy bulbs of thought sweat he listens
to the trees sparking conversations with the fields,
then the sound of a cattle truck splits the road,
the air for minutes hung and block-stained with
animal odour, then he is back to the why-wringing
of things, clasping his thought-hands as one, the
dreadnought of worry.

He is with faded shadows and there is moisture in the air,
somewhere lost fires spark a wanton winter, and elsewhere
ropes of midday sun sizzle on rusted red iron as a
sun-enamelled hill to the north and a rain-hitched slope
to the south watch the western wind cart desert dust to sea,
while a blue sky in spring handed summer morning heat
smiles at the rain that clings to a leaf as grass resting dunes
sun-drenched and heavy at sleep with sea salt miss the
sideways wobble of a crab and above seagulls' kite-glide
and admire a butterfly's tableau wings folding open,
quivering, closing, and then, he shivers with the
stippling brush of a sorrow kiss breeze at his neck.

Vistas – these portions of panoramas should be the backbone
of his happiness, the splints for his worried thoughts and that
breeze tatting at the arteries worming his temples should
convince and promise his pulse and heartbeat to echo peace at
his will but as day drifts into night passing over yesterday
he looks at the landscape, yet the cutlass of his gaze will
not allow him to decipher the trickery of the bush, its
settled tension, chaos cloaked as mystery and serenity,
that constant wheedling, calling him, beckoning – he feels its
warm calming embrace and breath, the wind and trees begin
applauding him and soon the road will adjust its camber
for a safer journey, forever drawing him on, questing him
to follow and as he listens one last time he can hear
Nature counting…

'Only strangers, the very poor and the dead walk in the bush.' – Les A. Murray
Comet is a town in Queensland.

A Blue Tinge in the Glass

'I am gone into the fields
To take what this sweet hour yields; –
Reflection, you may come to-morrow,
Sit by the fireside with Sorrow.' – P.B. Shelley

Your thoughts slanting,
squeezing my features back
through a moment of air,
your silver face of mist,
swallowing up my
jostling, ambling gait.

Avoiding my gaze, you
see your own deformity.

You mirror, speak face to
face, freely criticising.

My breath, never yours,
you cannot return it;
is lost on the flat scope
of your complexion.

Puffing a cloudy smudge,
the smear hurtles across
your watery surface,
your reply is but to watch me,
you are glib and for a moment
as the glass is clouded I forget
my crippled arms and bent legs.

Blinking, eyeing your clear skin,
I'm reminded once again that I'll never
be free of my body as you
will never be free of your
cold glassy junked memories,
stolen images loitering about behind
a false museum of solid watered glass.

There is a tinge of blue in your face, dear mirror.

What thoughts ink inside your head.

Night Has No Memory

In the line drawing of evening
chalk marks of last sunlight
sit coolly on the pavement.

As the tired sun nicotines west
facing windows a smattering of
rainbow lorikeets rim a copse of
wattles halter necking the branches.

Night awkwardly lonely as aspirin
coloured spots of rain milk the soil and
flying foxes crowbar the skyscape in
heavy rubbery sprung movement.

The moon like a gobbet of old flesh
stained linen sits in its catbird seat
watching an upset dog sage the
darkness as hitchhiker clouds mooch
and cloy, puzzling about as storm
shrouds vaccinate the western horizon.

The hours thrum, the slight hammering
of the street fluorescent like a dull pulse.

With faded feathers over time a bird
unbends the night with a callous screech.

Unlike elite archers who shoot between
heartbeats the city in its slow fizz of
mangoed light records slowly the
fingerprints left on the cookie-cutter
lives of people patrolling, persons
flavouring the tongued grooves of the
dark notes of emphasis in a city that
is never ever able to wallow in sleep.

Summer City Cycle

windows frown smiles glide
heat twirls building exits
crowds roam musing flowers
park bugs sky drapes
water wears ducks feathers
standing woman tradition indicates
eye cynic patronising glares
Joan of Arc thoughts
ideas collecting antique shop
corner creaking furniture lines
smug carpets touch of
dollars from hand on
to hand wooden feelings
carved in a summer
afternoon in the city.

Night Loneliness

Night air flavoured
with woodsmoke

a bird nowhere
shutters a guffawed cry

bad grass quantifies
the fenceline, openly

stars drip, the moon is
again drugged in cycle

the letter box flocked in
dew watches dreamily a

flying fox meandering
blackness, it's furred

wings stuck in yesterday
and in the sheer silence a

loud bark dogs the distance
a shed door moans squeaks

in the twisted wind and the old
church floorboards pray creak.

Dead Possum

Night-time: the skin of sky
pulled blackness tight.
I walk a bustle of breeze
at my back, my eyes
momentarily night-blind
then riddled with depth
and perspective, hunter's
eyes alone. With the
moon glow gone behind
the month's collar and
useless stars shining only
scatters of light I stop
and stand, my shoulders
swooped forward, I look.

Its body was all a wreck,
the end near the back legs
bulbous, full of stomached
air, the tail snapped in places
like a 'caught on film' image
of an exploding pressure
hose – some spots flat, others
erect with shape. The thing
did not move, its head bloodied
fur, eyes dark starred sapphires,
one ear almost off and a weak
'given in' grin split across its face.
I could have bundled the whole
mess in a kid's shoebox but instead
left it on its bitumen grave.

And in the morning with a
punishing sun beating its way
up a bleached blue sky, I realised
again no steel-belted tyre had
night fallen this furred animal.

And as I walked back, the sun
now curdling and sautéing the
body's insides I thought
suddenly and oddly
of Azaria Chamberlain.

Fumes Caught in a Net

Butterfly! These words
  from my brush
  are not flowers...
only their shadows.
                    Soseki

An interlace on loom of clouds
chalks the sky and the slimmest
breeze budges like a parachutist
fine adjusting in vacant air, the

speech of smoke over the waxy
mountains an intermixing of
sunlight and mist, stammering
afternoon pesters day, then an

old warrant for rain is yanked
from a farmer's thoughts and the
parched, peeled sun dribbles atop
Mount Warning like an orange on

a rhinoceros spike, ooze leaking
orange peel streaks, a rasp of
day moon chides air as pimple
rashes of pink pelmet the west,

a spider fish-hooks from a branch,
a thin frolic of line, a sun-dusted
anchoring rope, and away to the
south black epoxy clouds clutter,

litter the fading blueness like a
harem of black lilies veiling a pond.
their King Leared threats brewing,
our folk hero day moon like the

arced arm of a marksman and the
mountains miraged, distorted, filmic,
a gather of canoes itching over the
persimmon-stained sky horizon,

tall turpentine grass disentangles
itself from the stroked sunlight as
birds give speech to a half clap of
their wings and evening wires a

message that dew arrives tonight,
distant smoke queries the scene
giving a boxing blow harshness
of old whiteness, drying darkness

as the moon, its grey craters
like emptied kernels of wheat
ogles pensively like a Tibetan
monk salving the serenity, the

twill pattern of grass bending
bent over stuck together like
a cat's licked fur, the fields,
rusted with the sun's lace and

paddocks matted the colour of
old oak barrels sly watch the
rough log of mist tobogganing
the mountain's ribcage and as

in a dance of pain the stomach
settling powder of dusk slowly
picnic blankets the panorama,
the mountains boil as a left over

piece of sun atriums a trade of
clouds corroding a grassy hillside,
the sun syrup everywhere leaving
dog-print dabbings of glow across

the river silt flats, the droppings of
glow like acrobats fine tuning their
bindings into the turning darkness
that rests on a sheet of hot night, I

say goodbye to powdering wattles,
the flaking sunlight, to birds fluting
the heavens, to flame she-oaks that
run-sleep down the slope, to a set

of tapestried butterfly wings slow
quivering like webbed lichen and
down far off below, the ocean is a
choir of catacombs of waves with

cobwebs of froth all looking up at the
perched farmland ink-green pastures,
cattle cellophaning the fence line like
moveable targets, blank lolling eyes,

stoop walking, their silly moaning
groans enervating barbed wire like
fumes caught in a net, trees pitch
clear ridden moisture tents around

their bases as shadow and shade
call out to night, shadows genuflect
and like fallen mosaic tiles replaced
these shadows are hung incorrectly,

a rabbit run hops like in a skit and
insects tongue click, tap and jiggle,
I get up from the chair unmarried
to the black glossed night, with

ample day borrowed I realise that
I belong to an awareness of a
scheme of seeing and noticing,
nothing else and decades ago you

stationed in the old wicker chair
beside my bed saying don't be
scared of night, now I understand
that what gathers then unseals a

moment like a fused exhibit is the
lack of dreaming and not just the
remembering but the creating of
something from nothing, as though

things in each be snapshots of each
in echo, tonight your memories and
stories sweep back, yet the souvenirs
in your eyes are gone, no corn silt on

your hands, but you tighten the halter,
the reins, going off to check the gates,
watching the herd, the moonlight on
thistles wet with shivering dew, the

gasoline-coloured fog reptiling in
and you patrolling for dingoes and
as a sick bee sits atop a rock, dead
leaves and broken twigs watch as

the rocks remember the eulogies
of memories over sun blistered
cracked earth, the dogs of dust, the
curling fires black crossing the land,

the old cottage, the leadlight window
colours tourniqueted in glass in the
spent afternoon light, the cottage
collapsing over each wave cycle of

the fracturing sunlight and tonight a
design of stars, a reminder of your
troubles, pained times – a bracelet of
tears, a necklace full of dried scars,

white and brittled as old wormwood,
tonight closing your cottage door I
don't look back but I think I can hear
the swirls, whorls of the lasso loops

as you dear uncle, the embroider
of notebooks, inkwell lived ideas,
stories saucepanned into the fine
flavours of our family, you trick

corner gather another stray beast
for branding and the sounds of the
place echoed and stitched into my
memory like fumes caught in a net.

Just South of Echo

'Every lost landscape speaks its own story, like a strip of celluloid not often seen, as it is so devoid of human viewings, it self-discards itself like dust.'
– Ballantyne Fini

Night-skinned music playing
tall grass waving instinctively
the smell of tractor oil as
Indie goes to sleep, tonight
on the veranda I try to
centre stars against satellites,
like dull haloed moving
glint-blobs of sulphured light,
there is medicine in the dark,
the trees charcoal-filled sticks
on a coral-coloured paddock,
frost resting for a short while
before dribbling and the moon
throwing its cosmic glow across
a pre-wintered landscape,
Indie is asleep with slow
nightshade flicks of light-lime over
her hair-framed face, I scowl
with my eyes trying to dig
into slumber, then a nail file
breeze at the barn's west gate
the sound a bit like a small bird
pencilling my thoughts, booking
the moon's pearled glow ready for
an after show performance, chinked
stars canter the darkness and looking up

the sky fluttered with mothed cloud
those shaky stars resembling deep veins
of granite wailed into a rocked hillside
they notice the turpentine grass moving
strobingly to a shudder of dull lit night-wash,
unlike day's radiant eye itching light,
tonight everything is Moses ready,
insects and birds hike in their dreams
over settled cottages, misted mornings,
trawling heat in mid-afternoon and
later in the text of the year slow rob
their existence with the dry rot coolness
of winter, yet tonight there is a rising
damp of calmness like things floating.

The Woodblock Cutter

for 'N'

She works a piece of wood as I
wander with footsteps of thought.

Bushfires have riddled paddock fence
posts a fragile honeycombed brown-black.

She's cutting Iroquoian eastern white cedar
yet she'd prefer the cedars of Lebanon.

The stale breath of a day-old fire ekes from the chimney,
yard beasts with downed heads, eyes smoke wet and hazy
wearingly clump along the river's towpath, their
hair spot-burnt to flesh and as a horse nickers
and strolls in a still-green upper pasture the coming
cold damp might well slow-tension their pain.

Snow clouds short distance the horizon, purchase
the last loose bindings of sunlight and
cast it forlornly on a hillside ivied with regret.

The blade digs, rives, scrapes, her shoulders
wound inwards as she concentrates.

Her eyes capture intensity like they're
hanging torn inside a wild dog's head.

The narcotic effect of the ginger heat
of drying fading sunlight and the final
stickiness of dusk arriving alone.

This place is book pressed.

Curls of cedar fall, gather on the slate floor, dried
wildflowers devoid of their condiments of nectar.

Like a slow swarm darkness oscillates in, it chills a
dancing breeze against day's last shilly-shallying glow.

Goading the wood, scratching, paddling the chisel,
working both end grain and side grain, rasping.

Brushing, feathering each cut, perforation, cleaning like
an archaeologist moving striations of sediment from
the parched ribs of a dead-end river bed.

Creeping patterns eerily appear, disappear and reappear
like turned over fields of sorghum in a fleeing wind
some sections collapsed in relief, others upright,
porcupined in sharp panic.

Across this landscape come stuttering shadows
kneeling down to evening as night dithers
about in the travelling darkness.

Her most fond memory was the windmill,
her 'Mill of Wind' she'd called it,
now twisted, blackened and rattly.

Soon snowdrifts will fog-fur the windows.

New flames will charge the fireplace,
they will duck and dive, prance and purge,
their licking deer horn flames doing
silent drum loop movements.

We won't talk with our dry dried voices of
the wrinkled past, or of windrows of seaweed
or of the ruffled quilt of ocean or of the
dirtied bone-coloured snow, or of this place.

It is easy to fillet the words she does not speak,
by watching her hands.

They match the movement of flame on wood.

Only once does she look up, the orange-blue flames
reflected in her eyes, squinting into our future.

Like shearers capturing wool, flames work the wood,
logs strapped by heat and smoulder, black tuba sounds,
air funnelling along cracks, in and out of split ridges,
heat sucking and hissing at knots.

It is the black magic of burning talking to itself.

Now the windows fur-fogged and boxed in dreams.

There are no trumpets to put our little place into
eons of sleep, just old winter's darkness.

I sweep up curls, tendrils of shavings,
torn snake skin lengths, orts
and flip them into the heart of heat.

They spore the area with sparks.

It's Just a Photograph

It's just a photograph of the woman I love.
She's sitting on aluminium, a plank seat,

her hands that once opened her chest to view
now grip the gunwale curves, the water, frigid

lines running blue-grey away from the hull,
backwards, all tensioned up like gathers in a

skirt or weak-looking glass with those shudders
and ruffles of fractures just below the surface.

My eyes begin steering the shape of her bare feet,
her legs and her knees that are tightly together

taunting me, the blue floral dress just edging thighs,
but it's her legs that have me tracing, eye-touching

flesh, all the darkened little scars and booster
veins that trickle here and there, and looking up

her tongue is a little pink rudder moving slowly
across the warm slit of reddened lips, back and

across, her eyes like small hammers ready to
pin and tap my weak male needs, I push the oars

in, back over, and in, the sound of the water
like fingernails being drawn over satin sheets.

The Watcher

Southbank, Brisbane
'A poignant chaos was welling within me.' – *Lolita*, Vladimir Nabokov

Sweat shimmered and slipped
on his brow. This man with
woman-shaped thoughts eyed

the young girl. There was a
wheedling trickle of a note of
despair in her laughing voice

as she noticed him peering.
A breeze struck and swooped
at her fusty hair. He watched

with open clamshell eyes.
Other people with dull looks
like half asleep dogs never

noticed him leaning at the post.
The afternoon air was fuggy and
the gimcrackery of his smile as

the shadows argued and bustled
in this place of ardent shades.
His avid hands bunched in his

pockets, and those eyes transmitting
eager thoughts of how her flesh was
damp and spongy like a peeled banana.

Writing

I'm fashioning

a poem

fastening
to the page

with bent buckle
of iron thoughts

and cold-quartered
steel emotions

with racks of cloth
and freedom string

not in a glass bottle
on a desk but in

hell's rhythm at sea.

Camping

The tent
occasionally
flap buckles

with gusts,
the smell of
lavender and

mint and her
warm breath
at his neck,

a brown lizard
pushes its weight
in under moist

leaf litter as she
begins clawing
his back in spasms.

Old Photograph

'Having seen other fathers greet their sons,
I put my childish face up to be kissed. After
an absence. The rebuff still stuns my blood.' – James McAuley

In my laurel moments
I kiss your photograph,
proffered kisses sparking
my lips with a numbness.

Through the window
I watch rain dimple the
soft sand, rain falling
with its own weight
attached, each individual
drop by itself trying to

defy gravity or is rain like
a family where droplets
gather, cluster together
in a larger but weaker
mass, fast falling then
exploding like a clear

watermelon without a
parachute, this is of
course a silly thought
as I gaze once again
through the glass
lost droplets fall

from the branches,
it is right now at this
moment, at this very
moment, I think of you.

The Zoo

We'd been to the zoo, you'd
liked the wedge-tailed eagles
strut and upright stance, it

reminded you of your father
dancing, and you asked me
what I liked, I replied the
asphalt and humidity and
the stinging itchy heat,

you elbowed me in the ribs,
I said more honestly that I'd
liked the eagle's dark seedling

like eyes and his black steel
plumage but mostly I liked
when we kissed on the path
under the canopy of trees
between the snakes suffocating

heat on one side and the parrots
guffawing and rollicking about
on their perches watching us.

That Bike

for John Forbes

Leaving the Harold Park
after reading my final poem
Asbestos (dedicated to Sir
David Martin), the applause

was still hanging at the cleft
of my ears, the lights dabbing
at my back and you asking for
a lift. 4 people and a bike in a
Daihatsu Charade or 1 bike and
four people. The bike seemed
like an occurrence, a thing that
just happens on a late night in

Sydney. The drizzling rain
giving reason to everything.
That bike held on top by four
hands, knuckles choked white.

Frame our Determination

for Sup and John

'There's many a boy here today that looks upon war as all glory, but boys, it is all hell!' – William T. Sherman, 11 August 1880

As prompt and abrupt as a washed-up body on a foreign beach,
the stay wire, that tripwire of fear a tripwire at our feet – most
took off their boots trying to half-sleep, then in pulling darkness,
a slow night where any glow had burnt out, had gone they came,
they came to play, to tickle our toes like piano keys, to tap rub
the underside of our feet, the ankle bone, sometimes whiskering
our chin with the gun's heavy cold steel end, up and across, until
we snapped sudden awake, the young ones had reflex but us
older guys had guile, having seen death's scowl we were a bit
more wile, but still they came, at times cautionary themselves,

wary of Aussie diggers half sleeping, catnapping their trigger,
two bolts of death meeting barrel to barrel, with another just
waiting in line in dark's troubled heart – the fear slotted into
your eyes, plugged deep into muscles, tattooed into your spine
fear like iced steel wet with sharpness, your blood hot and sticky
and in the jungle clearing your wide-open eyes notice nothing,
it is in these fragiled moments that you pray, and ask God does
he weep and eye rub, does he wonder, we can't see or hear him
but he's there in these impossible freeze-frame drawn-out times

he's picture framing our determination, was he there when I
stepped from behind the school bus, the bevelled edge of the
framed glass reflecting, yearning my safety as the errant car
swerved and sped off, there are no sermons remembered as
faith is an intense prayer about the moment, no time for cheap
heroed thoughts, false machismo, bravado or flexed egos
polished in anger, you pray by asking, thinking of life, you
can't win a war blindfolded to an enemy's angered reason;
they came to tickle our stanching feet, the feathering touch

of steel in the steamy black, no moonlit edge to the barrel,
just its raw presence, its deathly purpose, the military life of
a gun, the bullets journeying at our eyeline, at our growth
of sight in early morning, perhaps the snap sudden click,
pause, then gone, fleeting footstep movements pacing away
or perhaps nothing but that reminder of the hesitation, a
blistered memory of the event, darker, truer each and every
Anzac Day with the re-echoes of decades of us being
unwelcome because we were Vietnam Vets and yet some

of us had learnt through the sheer hatred, guttural detest
and razor-sharp fear to lie awake, wait, pistol resting childlike
at our chest or the rifle walking-stick like, a third leg, listening
for the crunch of jungle flooring, a smell of movement, a
cunningness surrounding your resting shape, an X-ray image
darkly moving in shouldered silence, in the solid air, your spine
stiff like a stuck-open gate, you watch for the first show of a
darker darkness, then the sudden inch lifting and pulling of
trigger, the event replayed over and over in the mind's hollowed-
out hall of voices, heard and unheard all through the night.

Acknowledgements

'Woodsmoke and Ash' was Highly Commended in the W.B. Yeats Poetry Prize and in the John Shaw Neilson Poetry Award, and Commended in the Gregory O'Donoghue International Poetry Competition.

'A Litter of Seven' won 2nd Prize in the John Shaw Neilson Poetry Award and was Commended in the W.B. Yeats Poetry Prize and in the Gregory O'Donoghue International Poetry Competition.

'Teardrops on a Feather' won 2nd Prize in the Shoalhaven Literary Award.

'Lions and Inscriptions' was shortlisted for the Lane Cove Literary Award and for the Joseph Furphy Commemorative Poetry Prize, and Commended in the Patron's Prize for Poetry.

'Like a Diving Bell Fathom Dropping' won 2nd Prize in the Glen Phillips Poetry Prize.

'The Cold Stones of Feeling' won 3rd Prize in the KSP Poetry Award and was Commended in the John Shaw Neilson Poetry Award.

'High Country, Australian Alps' won the Lane Cove Literary Award.

'Stage Whispers' won the Bruce Dawe National Poetry Prize and was Highly Commended in the W.B. Yeats Poetry Prize.

'Ticking Again' won 3rd Prize in the Ron Pretty Poetry Prize.

'Detention' was Highly Commended in the W.B. Yeats Poetry Prize and Commended in the Gregory O'Donoghue International Poetry Competition.

'The Trawler' was shortlisted in the Newcastle Poetry Prize.

'*Nacht und Nebel*' was Highly Commended in the W.B. Yeats Poetry Prize.

'The Bat, the Bell, the Bird and the Body' was longlisted for the Montreal Poetry Prize.

'You Are Gone' won the Adrien Abbott Poetry Prize.

'Summer Night Writing' was shortlisted for the Joseph Furphy Commemorative Poetry Prize and Commended in the Gregory O'Donoghue International Poetry Competition.

'Fragment's was published in the Poetica Christi Press anthology and Commended in the Gregory O'Donoghue International Poetry Competition.

'Chateau de Lavigny, Switzerland' was published in the Poetica Christi Press anthology and Commended in the Gregory O'Donoghue International Poetry Competition.

'Salute' was Commended in the W.B. Yeats Poetry Prize.

'The Long House' was shortlisted for the Right Now Human Rights Poetry Award.

'Fallen Leaves' was Highly Commended in the W.B. Yeats Poetry Prize and Commended in the Gregory O'Donoghue International Poetry Competition.

'The Rhythm Line' was Commended in the Gregory O'Donoghue International Poetry Competition and published in the Poetica Christi Press anthology.

'Compass' was Commended in the Gregory O'Donoghue International Poetry Competition.

'On the Road Outside Comet' was runner-up in the UQ Vanguard Literary Award, shortlisted in the Newcastle Poetry Prize and published in *Heat*.

'A Tinge of Blue in the Glass' was Commended in the Gregory O'Donoghue International Poetry Competition.

'Summer City Cycle' was Commended in the FAW Tasmania Poetry Prize.

'Dead Possum' was Commended in the Liz Huff Memorial Poetry Award.

'Fumes Caught in a Net' was Commended in the Gregory O'Donoghue International Poetry Competition.

'Just South of Echo' was Commended in the Ros Spencer Poetry Prize and published in the *Ros Spencer Poetry Prize* Anthology.

'It's Just a Photograph' was published in *Blast*.

'The Watcher' was Highly Commended in the Ipswich International Poetry Prize and Highly Commended in the R.T. Edwards Poetry Award.

'Writing' was published in *Eureka Street*.

'Camping' was published in *The Weekend Australian*.

'Old Photograph' won the C.J. Dennis Literary Award.

'The Zoo' won the Beech Hedges Poetry Award and won the C.J. Dennis Literary Award.

'That Bike' was published in *FourW*.

'Frame Our Determination' was published in *When Anzac Day Comes Around – 100 years from Gallipoli Poetry Project*.

www.ingramcontent.com/pod-product-compliance
Lightning Source LLC
Chambersburg PA
CBHW062141100526
44589CB00014B/1646